GW01374701

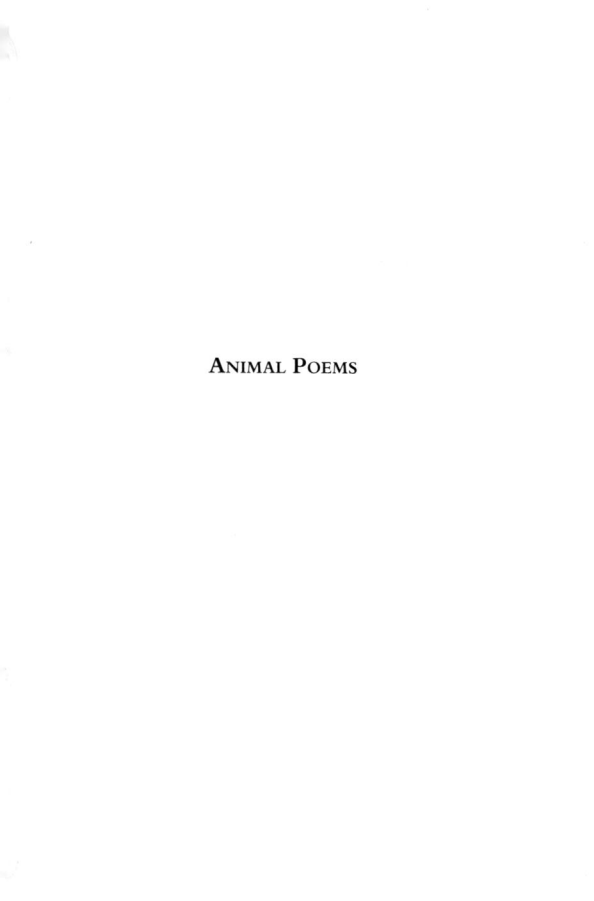

Animal Poems

JARROLD POETS SERIES

Also in this series:

Robert and Elizabeth Browning
Robert Burns
Lord Byron
Samuel Taylor Coleridge
John Keats
Rudyard Kipling
The Lady Poets
Scottish Poems & Ballads
Percy Bysshe Shelley
Alfred, Lord Tennyson
The War Poets
William Wordsworth
Childhood Poems
Love Poems
Pastoral Poems
Patriotic Poems
Sea Poems

ANIMAL POEMS – AN ANTHOLOGY

Poems selected by Anne Priestley
Designed by Parke Sutton Publishing Limited
for Jarrold Publishing, Norwich
First published 1994

ISBN 0-7117-0676-X

CONTENTS

ANONYMOUS
The Swan 9
SIR PHILIP SIDNEY (1554–1586)
From: Second Eclogues of Arcadia 10
ROBERT HERRICK (1591–1674)
His Grange, or Private Wealth 11
JOHN BUNYAN (1628–88)
Upon the Snail 13
THOMAS GRAY (1716–71)
Ode on the Death of a Favourite Cat, Drowned
  in a Tub of Gold Fishes 14
WILLIAM BLAKE (1757–1827)
The Lamb 17
The Tiger 18
JOHN HOOKHAM FRERE (1769–1846)
The Boy and the Parrot 20
WILLIAM WORDSWORTH (1770–1850)
The Kitten and Falling Leaves 22
ANONYMOUS
Noah, Sailing o'er the Seas 24

WILLIAM WORDSWORTH (1770–1850)
To the Cuckoo 25
ROBERT SOUTHEY (1774–1843)
To a Goose. 27
LEIGH HUNT (1784–1859)
The Grasshopper and the Cricket 28
Three Sonnets 29
JOHN CLARE (1793–1864)
The Thrush's Nest 32
SAMUEL TAYLOR COLERIDGE (1772–1834)
Answer to a Child's Question 33
ANONYMOUS
The Wren 34
RICHARD SCRAFTON SHARPE (1775?–1852)
The Country Mouse and the City Mouse 35
PERCY BYSSHE SHELLEY (1792–1822)
To a Skylark 38
RICHARD HARRIS BARHAM (THOMAS INGOLDSBY)
(1788–1845)
The Jackdaw of Rheims 44
JOHN KEATS (1795–1821)
To a Cat. 52
The Grasshopper and Cricket 53

MARY HOWITT (1799–1888)
The Spider and the Fly 54
EDGAR ALLAN POE (1809–49)
The Raven 58
ALFRED, LORD TENNYSON (1809–92)
The Eagle 66
Song: The Owl 67
AUNT EFFIE (JANE EUPHEMIA BROWNE) (1811–98)
The Great Brown Owl 68
EDWARD LEAR (1812–88)
The Duck and the Kangaroo 69
The Owl and the Pussy Cat 72
ELIZA COOK (1818–89)
The Mouse and the Cake 74
CECIL FRANCES ALEXANDER (1818–95)
The Fieldmouse 76
EMILY DICKINSON (1830–86)
A Bird Came Down the Walk 78
A Narrow Fellow in the Grass 80
CHRISTINA ROSSETTI (1830–94)
The Caterpillar 82
The Horses of the Sea 82

Lewis Carroll (1832–98)
How Doth the Little Crocodile 83
The Walrus and the Carpenter 84
Richard Garnett (1835–1906)
Marigold 90
Thomas Hardy (1840–1928)
The Oxen 91
Charles E. Carryl (1841–1920)
The Camel's Complaint 92
A.E. Housman (1859–1936)
The Elephant, or The Force of Habit 94
Kenneth Grahame (1859–1931)
Ducks' Ditty 95
John Davidson (1857–1909)
A Runnable Stag 97
Rudyard Kipling (1865–1936)
The Law of the Jungle 102
How the Camel Got His Hump 106
From: The Cat That Walked by Himself 108
W.B. Yeats (1865–1939)
The Cat and the Moon 110
The Wild Swans at Coole 112

G.K. CHESTERTON (1874–1936)
The Donkey 114
Triolet 115
VACHEL LINDSAY (1879–1931)
The Flower-fed Buffaloes 116
JOHN DRINKWATER (1882–1937)
Snail 117
D.H. LAWRENCE (1885–1930)
Humming-bird 118
Snake 119
HUMBERT WOLFE (1885–1940)
The Blackbird 124
The Grey Squirrel 125
ELIZABETH MADOX ROBERTS (1885–1941)
The Hens 126
JULIAN GRENFELL (1888–1915)
To a Black Greyhound 127

ANONYMOUS

THE SWAN

Translated from the Old English

My robe is noiseless while I tread the earth,
Or tarry 'neath the banks, or stir the shallows;
But when these shining wings, this depth of air,
Bear me aloft above the bending shores
Where men abide, and far the welkin's strength
Over the multitudes conveys me, then
With rushing whir and clear melodious sound
My raiment sings. And like a wandering spirit
I float unweariedly o'er flood and field.

Sir Philip Sidney

From: Second Eclogues of Arcadia

I have (and long shall have) a white great nimble cat,
A king upon a mouse, a strong foe to the rat,
Fine eares, long taile he hath, with Lions curbed clawe,
Which oft he lifteth up, and stayes his lifted pawe,
Deepe musing to himselfe, which after-mewing showes,
Till with lickt beard, his eye of fire espie his foes.

Robert Herrick

His grange, or Private Wealth

Though Clock,
To tell how night drawes hence, I've none,
A Cock,
I have, to sing how day drawes on.
I have
A maid (my Prew*) by good luck sent,*
To save
That little, Fates me gave or lent.
A Hen
I keep, which creeking day by day,
Tells when
She goes her long white egg to lay.
A Goose
I have, which, with a jealous eare,
Lets loose
Her tongue, to tell what danger's neare.
A Lamb
I keep (tame) with my morsells fed,
Whose Dam
An Orphan left him (lately dead).
A Cat

I keep, that playes about my House,
    Grown fat,
With eating many a miching Mouse.
    To these
A Trasy I do keep, whereby
    I please
The more my rurall privacie:
    Which are
But toyes, to give my heart some ease:
    Where care
None is, slight things do lightly please.

JOHN BUNYAN

UPON THE SNAIL

She goes but softly, but she goeth sure;
She stumbles not as stronger creatures do:
Her journey's shorter, so she may endure
Better than they which do much further go.

She makes no noise, but stilly seizeth on
The flower or herb appointed for her food,
The which she quietly doth feed upon.
While others range, and gare, but find no good.

And though she doth but very softly go,
However 'tis not fast, nor slow, but sure;
And certainly they that do travel so,
The prize they do aim at they do procure.

Thomas Gray

Ode on the Death of a Favourite Cat, Drowned in a Tub of Gold Fishes

'Twas on a lofty vase's side,
Where China's gayest art had dyed
   The azure flowers, that blow;
Demurest of the tabby kind,
The pensive Selima reclined,
   Gazed on the lake below.

Her conscious tail her joy declared,
The fair round face, the snowy beard,
   The velvet of her paws,
Her coat, that with the tortoise vies,
Her ears of jet and emerald eyes,
   She saw, and purred applause.

Still had she gazed but 'midst the tide
Two angel forms were seen to glide,
   The Genii of the stream;
Their scaly armour's Tyrian hue
Through richest purple to the view
   Betrayed a golden gleam.

The hapless nymph with wonder saw:
A whisker first and then a claw,
With many an ardent wish,
She stretched in vain to reach the prize.
What female heart can gold despise?
What cat's averse to fish?

Presumptuous maid! with looks intent
Again she stretched, again she bent,
Nor knew the gulf between.
(Malignant Fate sat by, and smiled)
The slippery verge her feet beguiled,
She tumbled headlong in.

Eight times emerging from the flood
She mewed to every watry god,
Some speedy aid to send.
No dolphin came, no Nereid stirred:
Nor cruel Tom, nor Susan heard.
A favourite has no friend!

From hence, ye beauties, undeceived,
Know, one false step is ne'er retrieved,
    And be with caution bold.
Not all that tempts your wandering eyes
And heedless hearts, is lawful prize;
    Nor all that glisters, gold.

William Blake
The Lamb

Little lamb, who made thee?
Dost thou know who made thee?
Gave thee life, and bid thee feed
By the stream and o'er the mead;
Gave thee clothing of delight,
Softest clothing, woolly, bright;
Gave thee such a tender voice,
Making all the vales rejoice?
Little lamb, who made thee?
Dost thou know who made thee?

Little lamb, I'll tell thee;
Little lamb, I'll tell thee;
He is callèd by thy name,
For He calls Himself a Lamb,
He is meek, and he is mild,
He became a little child,
I a child, and thou a lamb
We are called by his name.
Little lamb, God bless thee!
Little lamb, God bless thee!

WILLIAM BLAKE

THE TIGER

Tiger! Tiger! burning bright
In the forests of the night,
What immortal hand or eye
Could frame thy fearful symmetry?

In what distant deeps or skies
Burnt the fire of thine eyes?
On what wings dare he aspire?
What the hand dare seize the fire?

And what shoulder, and what art
Could twist the sinews of thy heart?
And, when thy heart began to beat,
What dread hand, and what dread feet?

What the hammer? what the chain?
In what furnace was thy brain?
What the anvil? what dread grasp
Dare its deadly terrors clasp?

When the stars threw down their spears,
And water'd heaven with their tears,
Did he smile his work to see?
Did he who made the lamb make thee?

Tiger! Tiger! burning bright
In the forests of the night,
What immortal hand or eye
Dare frame thy fearful symmetry?

John Hookham Frere
The Boy and the Parrot

*"Parrot, if I had your wings
I should do so many things:
The first thing I should like to do
If I had little wings like you,
I should fly to Uncle Bartle,
Don't you think 'twould make him startle,
If he saw me when I came,
Flapping at the window frame
Exactly like the parrot of fame?"*

*All this the wise old parrot heard,
The parrot was an ancient bird,
And paused and pondered every word;
First, therefore, he began to cough,
Then said, "It is a great way off,
A great way off, my dear"; and then
He paused awhile, and coughed again:
"Master John, pray think a little,
What will you do for beds and victual?"*

"Oh! parrot, Uncle John can tell –
But we should manage very well;
At night we'd perch upon the trees,
And so fly forward by degrees."

"Does Uncle John", the parrot said,
"Put nonsense in his nephew's head?
Instead of telling you such things,
And teaching you to wish for wings,
I think he might have taught you better,
You might have learnt to write a letter:
That is the thing that I should do
If I had little hands like you."

William Wordsworth

The Kitten and Falling Leaves

See the Kitten on the wall,
Sporting with the leaves that fall,
Withered leaves – one – two – and three –
From the lofty elder-tree!
Through the calm and frosty air
Of this morning bright and fair,
Each invisible and mute,
In his wavering parachute.

– But the Kitten, how she starts,
Crouches, stretches, paws, and darts!
First at one, and then its fellow,
Just as light and just as yellow;
There are many now – now one –
Now they stop and there are none:
What intenseness of desire
In her upward eye of fire!

With a tiger-leap half-way
Now she meets the coming prey,
Lets it go as fast, and then
Has it in her power again.
Now she works with three or four,
Like an Indian conjurer;
Quick as he in feats of art,
Far beyond in joy of heart.

Anonymous

Noah, Sailing o'er the Seas

Noah, sailing o'er the seas
Ran fast aground on Ararat,
His dog then made a spring and took
The tail from off a pretty cat;
Puss through the window quick did fly,
And bravely through the waters swam
Nor ever stopped till high and dry,
She landed on the Calf of Man.
Thus tailless Puss earned Mona's thanks
And ever after was called Manx.

WILLIAM WORDSWORTH
To the Cuckoo

Oh Blithe New-Comer! I have heard,
I hear thee and rejoice,
O Cuckoo! shall I call thee Bird,
Or but a wandering Voice?

While I am lying on the grass
Thy twofold shout I hear,
From hill to hill it seems to pass,
At once far off, and near.

Though babbling only to the Vale,
Of sunshine and of flowers,
Thou bringest unto me a tale
Of visionary hours.

Thrice welcome, darling of the Spring!
Even yet thou art to me
No bird, but an invisible thing,
A voice, a mystery;

*The same whom in my school-boy days
I listened to; that Cry
Which made me look a thousand ways
In bush, and tree, and sky.*

*To seek thee did I often rove
Through woods and on the green;
And thou wert still a hope, a love;
Still longed for, never seen.*

*And I can listen to thee yet;
Can lie upon the plain
And listen, till I do beget
That golden time again.*

*O blessed Bird! the earth we pace
Again appears to be
An unsubstantial, faery place;
That is fit home for Thee!*

Robert Southey

To a Goose

If thou didst feed on western plains of yore;
Or waddle wide with flat and flabby feet
Over some Cambrian mountain's plashy moor;
Or find in farmer's yard a safe retreat
From gipsy thieves, and foxes sly and fleet;
If thy grey quills, by lawyer guided, trace
Deeds big with ruin to some wretched race,
Or love-sick poet's sonnet, sad and sweet,
Wailing the rigour of his lady fair;
Or if, the drudge of housemaid's daily toil,
Cobwebs and dust thy pinions white besoil,
Departed Goose! I neither know nor care.
But this I know, that we pronounced thee fine,
Seasoned with sage and onions, and port wine.

Leigh Hunt

The Grasshopper and the Cricket

Green little vaulter in the sunny grass,
  Catching your heart up at the feel of June,
  Sole voice that's heard amidst the lazy noon,
When even the bees lag at the summoning brass; –
And you, warm little housekeeper, who class
  With those who think the candles come too soon,
  Loving the fire, and with your tricksome tune
Nick the glad silent moments as they pass; –

O sweet and tiny cousins, that belong,
  One to the fields, the other to the hearth,
Both have your sunshine; both, though small, are strong
  At your clear hearts; and both seem given to earth
To sing in thoughtful ears this natural song –
  Indoors and out, – summer and winter, – Mirth.

LEIGH HUNT

THREE SONNETS

I

TO A FISH

You strange, astonished-looking, angle-faced,
Dreary-mouthed, gaping wretches of the sea,
Gulping salt water everlastingly,
Cold-blooded, though with red your blood be graced,
And mute, though dwellers in the roaring waste;
And you, all shapes beside, that fishy be –
Some round, some flat, some long, all devilry,
Legless, unloving, infamously chaste:

O scaly, slippery, wet, swift, staring wights,
What is't ye do? What life lead? eh, dull goggles?
How do ye vary your vile days and nights?
How pass your Sundays? Are ye still but joggles
In ceaseless wash? Still nought but gapes, and bites,
And drinks, and stares, diversified with boggles?

II

A Fish Replies

Amazing monster! that, for aught I know,
With the first sight of thee didst make our race
For ever stare! O flat and shocking face,
Grimly divided from the breast below!
Thou that on dry land horribly dost go
With a split body and most ridiculous pace,
Prong after prong, disgracer of all grace,
Long-useless-finned, haired, upright, unwet, slow!

O breather of unbreathable, sword-sharp air,
How canst exist? How bear thyself, thou dry
And dreary sloth? What particle canst share
Of the only blessed life, the watery?
I sometimes see of ye an actual pair
Go by, linked fin by fin, most odiously.

III

THE FISH TURNS INTO A MAN, AND THEN INTO A SPIRIT, AND AGAIN SPEAKS

Indulge thy smiling scorn, if smiling still,
O man! and loathe, but with a sort of love;
For difference must its use by difference prove,
And, in sweet clang, the spheres with music fill.
One of the spirits am I, that at his will
Live in whate'er has life – fish, eagle, dove –
No hate, no pride, beneath naught, nor above,
A visitor of the rounds of God's sweet skill.

Man's life is warm, glad, sad, 'twixt loves and graves,
Boundless in hope, honoured with pangs austere,
Heaven-gazing; and his angel-wings he craves:
The fish is swift, small-needing, vague yet clear,
A cold, sweet, silver life, wrapped in round waves,
Quickened with touches of transporting fear.

John Clare

The Thrush's Nest

Within a thick and spreading hawthorn bush,
That overhung a molehill large and round,
I heard from morn to morn a merry thrush
Sing hymns to sunrise, and I drank the sound
With joy; and often, an intruding guest,
I watched her secret toil from day to day
How true she warped the moss, to form a nest,
And modelled it within with wood and clay;
And by-and-by, like heath bells gilt with dew,
There lay her shining eggs, as bright as flowers,
Ink-spotted over shells of greeny blue;
And there I witnessed in the sunny hours,
A brood of Nature's minstrels chirp and fly,
Glad as the sunshine and the laughing sky.

Samuel Taylor Coleridge
Answer to a Child's Question

Do you ask what the birds say? The Sparrow, the Dove,
The Linnet and Thrush say, "I love and I love!"
In the winter they're silent – the wind is so strong;
What it says, I don't know, but it sings a loud song.
But green leaves, and blossoms, and sunny warm
   weather,
And singing, and loving – all come back together.
But the Lark is so brimful of gladness and love,
The green fields below him, the blue sky above,
That he sings, and he sings; and for ever sings he –
"I love my Love, and my Love loves me!"

Anonymous

The Wren

The little Wren of tender mind,
To every other bird is kind;
It ne'er to mischief bends its will,
But sings and is good-humoured still.
Whoe'er has mixed in childish play
Must sure have heard the children say,
"The Robin and the Jenny Wren
Are God Almighty's cock and hen."
Hence 'tis from all respect they meet,
Hence all in kindly manner treat;
For none would use with disrespect,
Whom Heaven thinks proper to protect.

Richard Scrafton Sharpe

The Country Mouse and the City Mouse

In a snug little cot lived a fat little mouse,
Who enjoyed, unmolested, the range of the house;
With plain food content, she would breakfast on cheese,
She dined upon bacon, and supped on grey peas.

A friend from the town to the cottage did stray,
And he said he was come a short visit to pay;
So the mouse spread her table as gay as you please,
And brought the nice bacon and charming grey peas.

The visitor frowned, and he thought to be witty:
Cried he, "You must know, I am come from the city,
Where we all should be shocked at provisions like these,
For we never eat bacon and horrid grey peas.

"To town come with me, I will give you a treat:
Some excellent food, most delightful to eat.
With me shall you feast just as long as you please;
Come, leave this fat bacon and shocking grey peas."

This kind invitation she could not refuse,
And the city mouse wished not a moment to lose;
Reluctant she quitted the fields and the trees,
The delicious fat bacon and charming grey peas.

They slily crept under a gay parlour door,
Where a feast had been given the evening before;
And it must be confessed they on dainties did seize,
Far better than bacon, or even grey peas.

Here were custard and trifle, and cheesecakes good store,
Nice sweetmeats and jellies, and twenty things more;
All that art had invented the palate to please,
Except some fat bacon and smoking grey peas.

They were nicely regaling, when into the room
Came the dog and the cat, and the maid with a broom:
They jumped in a custard both up to their knees;
The country mouse sighed for her bacon and peas.

*Cried she to her friend, "Get me safely away,
I can venture no longer in London to stay;
For if oft you receive interruptions like these,
Give me my nice bacon and charming grey peas.*

*"Your living is splendid and gay, to be sure,
But the dread of disturbance you ever endure;
I taste true delight in contentment and ease,
And I feast on fat bacon and charming grey peas."*

Percy Bysshe Shelley

To a Skylark

Hail to thee, blithe Spirit!
  Bird thou never wert,
That from Heaven, or near it,
  Pourest thy full heart
In profuse strains of unpremeditated art.

Higher still and higher
  From the earth thou springest
Like a cloud of fire;
  The blue deep thou wingest,
And singing still dost soar, and soaring ever singest.

In the golden lightning
  Of the sunken sun,
O'er which clouds are bright'ning,
  Thou dost float and run;
Like an unbodied joy whose race is just begun.

The pale purple even
  Melts around thy flight;
Like a star of Heaven,
  In the broad daylight
Thou art unseen, but yet I hear thy shrill delight,

Keen as are the arrows
  Of that silver sphere,
Whose intense lamp narrows
  In the white dawn clear
Until we hardly see – we feel that it is there.

All the earth and air
  With thy voice is loud,
As, when night is bare,
  From one lonely cloud
The moon rains out her beams, and Heaven is overflowed.

What thou art we know not;
  What is most like thee?
From rainbow clouds there flow not
  Drops so bright to see
As from thy presence showers a rain of melody.

Like a Poet hidden
  In the light of thought,
Singing hymns unbidden,
  Till the world is wrought
To sympathy with hopes and fears it heeded not:

Like a high-born maiden
  In a palace-tower,
Soothing her love-laden
  Soul in secret hour
With music sweet as love, which overflows her bower:

Like a glow-worm golden
  In a dell of dew,
Scattering unbeholden
  Its aëreal hue
Among the flowers and grass, which screen it from the view!

Like a rose embowered
  In its own green leaves,
By warm winds deflowered,
  Till the scent it gives

Makes faint with too much sweet those heavy-wingèd
  thieves:

Sound of vernal showers
  On the twinkling grass,
Rain-awakened flowers,
  All that ever was
Joyous, and clear, and fresh, thy music doth surpass:

Teach us, Sprite or Bird,
  What sweet thoughts are thine:
I have never heard
  Praise of love or wine
That panted forth a flood of rapture so divine.

Chorus Hymeneal,
  Or triumphal chant,
Matched with thine would be all
  But an empty vaunt,
A thing wherein we feel there is some hidden want.

What objects are the fountains
  Of thy happy strain?

What fields, or waves, or mountains?
    What shapes of sky or plain?
What love of thine own kind? what ignorance of pain?

With thy clear keen joyance
    Languor cannot be:
Shadow of annoyance
    Never came near thee:
Thou lovest – but ne'er knew love's sad satiety.

Waking or asleep,
    Thou of death must deem
Things more true and deep
    Than we mortals dream,
Or how could thy notes flow in such a crystal stream?

We look before and after,
    And pine for what is not:
Our sincerest laughter
    With some pain is fraught;
Our sweetest songs are those that tell of saddest thought.

Yet if we could scorn
    Hate, and pride, and fear;
If we were things born
    Not to shed a tear,
I know not how thy joy we ever should come near.

Better than all measures
    Of delightful sound,
Better than all treasures
    That in books are found,
Thy skill to poet were, thou scorner of the ground!

Teach me half the gladness
    That thy brain must know,
Such harmonious madness
    From my lips would flow
The world should listen then – as I am listening now.

Richard Harris Barham
(Thomas Ingoldsby)
The Jackdaw of Rheims

The Jackdaw sat on the Cardinal's chair!
Bishop and abbot and prior were there;
Many a monk and many a friar,
Many a knight and many a squire,
With a great many more of lesser degree, –
In sooth a goodly company;
And they served the Lord Primate on bended knee.
Never I ween
Was a prouder seen,
Read of in books, or dreamt of in dreams,
Than the Cardinal Lord Archbishop of Rheims!

In and out
Through the motley rout,
That little Jackdaw kept hopping about;
Here and there
Like a dog in a fair,
Over comfits and cates,
And dishes and plates,

Cowl and cope, and rochet and pall,
Mitre and crosier! he hopp'd upon all!
   With saucy air,
   He perch'd on the chair
Where, in state, the great Lord Cardinal sat
In the great Lord Cardinal's great red hat.
   And he peer'd in the face
   Of his Lordship's Grace
With a satisfied look, as if he would say,
"We two are the greatest folks here to-day!"
   And the priests, with awe,
   As such freaks they saw,
Said, "The Devil must be in that little Jackdaw!"

The feast was over. The board was clear'd.
The flawns and the custards had all disappear'd.
And six little singing-boys, – dear little souls!
In nice clean faces, and nice white stoles,
   Came, in order due,
   Two by two,
Marching that grand refectory through!
A nice little boy held a golden ewer,
Emboss'd and fill'd with water, as pure
As any that flows between Rheims and Namur,

*Which a nice little boy stood ready to catch
In a fine golden hand-basin made to match.
Two nice little boys, rather more grown,
Carried lavender-water, and eau de Cologne;
And a nice little boy had a nice cake of soap,
Worthy of washing the hands of the Pope.*
 *One little boy more
 A napkin bore
Of the best white diaper, fringed with pink,
And a Cardinal's Hat mark'd in permanent ink.*

*The great Lord Cardinal turns at the sight
Of these nice little boys dress'd all in white.
 From his finger he draws
 His costly turquoise;
And, not thinking at all about little Jackdaws,
 Deposits it straight
 By the side of his plate,
While the nice little boys on his Eminence wait;
Till, when nobody's dreaming of any such thing,
That little Jackdaw hops off with the ring!*

 *There's a cry and a shout,
 And a deuce of a rout,*

And nobody seems to know what they're about,
But the monks have their pockets all turn'd inside out.
  The friars are kneeling,
  And hunting, and feeling
The carpet, the floor, and the walls, and the ceiling.
  The Cardinal drew
  Off each plum-colour'd shoe,
And left his red stockings exposed to the view;
  He peeps, and he feels
  In the toes and the heels.
They turn up the dishes. They turn up the plates.
They take up the poker and poke out the grates.
  They turn up the rugs.
  They examine the mugs.
  But, no! – no such thing; –
  They can't find THE RING!
And the Abbot declared that, "when nobody twigg'd it,
Some rascal or other had popp'd in, and prigg'd it!"

The Cardinal rose with a dignified look.
He call'd for his candle, his bell, and his book!
  In holy anger and pious grief
  He solemnly cursed that rascally thief!
  He cursed him at board, he cursed him in bed,

From the sole of his foot to the crown of his head;
He cursed him in sleeping, that every night
He should dream of the devil, and wake in a fright;
He cursed him in eating, he cursed him in drinking,
He cursed him in coughing, in sneezing, in winking;
He cursed him in sitting, in standing, in lying;
He cursed him in walking, in riding, in flying,
He cursed him in living, he cursed him in dying! –
Never was heard such a terrible curse!
    But what gave rise
    To no little surprise –
Nobody seem'd one penny the worse!

    The day was gone.
    The night came on.
The Monks and the Friars they search'd till dawn,
    When the Sacristan saw,
    On crumpled claw,
Come limping a poor little lame Jackdaw!
    No longer gay,
    As on yesterday;
His feathers all seem'd to be turn'd the wrong way; –
His pinions droop'd – he could hardly stand, –
His head was as bald as the palm of your hand;

His eyes so dim,
  So wasted each limb,
That, heedless of grammar, they all cried, "THAT'S HIM!" –
That's the scamp that has done this scandalous thing!
That's the thief that has got my Lord Cardinal's Ring!"
  The poor little Jackdaw,
  When the Monks he saw,
Feebly gave vent to the ghost of a caw;
And turn'd his bald head, as much as to say,
"Pray, be so good as to walk this way!"
  Slower and slower
  He limp'd on before,
Till they came to the back of the belfry door,
  Where the first thing they saw,
  Midst the sticks and the straw,
Was the RING in the nest of that little Jackdaw!

Then the great Lord Cardinal call'd for his book
And off that terrible curse he took.
  The mute expression
  Served in lieu of confession,
And, being thus coupled with full restitution,
The Jackdaw got plenary absolution!

  — When those words were heard,
  That poor little bird
Was so changed in a moment, 'twas really absurd.
  He grew sleek, and fat.
  In addition to that,
A fresh crop of feathers came thick as a mat!

  His tail waggled more
  Even than before.
But no longer it wagg'd with an impudent air.
No longer he perch'd on the Cardinal's chair.
  He hopp'd now about
  With a gait devout.
At Matins, at Vespers, he never was out.
And, so far from any more pilfering deeds,
He always seem'd telling the Cónfessor's beads.
If any one lied, — or if any one swore, —
Or slumber'd in prayer-time and happen'd to snore,

    That good Jackdaw
    Would give a great 'Caw!'
As much as to say, "Don't do so any more!"
While many remark'd, as his manners they saw,
That they "never had known such a pious Jackdaw!"
    He long lived the pride
    Of that country-side,
And at last in the odour of sanctity died;
    When, as words were too faint
    His merits to paint,
The Conclave determined to make him a Saint;
And on newly made Saints and Popes, as you know,
It's the custom, at Rome, new names to bestow,
So they canonised him by the name of 'Jim Crow'!

John Keats
To a Cat

Cat! who has pass'd thy grand climacteric,
How many mice and rats hast in thy days
Destroy'd – How many tit bits stolen? Gaze
With those bright languid segments green, and prick
Those velvet ears – but pr'ythee do not stick
Thy latent talons in me – and upraise
Thy gentle mew – and tell me all thy frays
Of fish and mice, and rats and tender chick.
Nay, look not down, nor lick thy dainty wrists –
For all the wheezy asthma, – and for all
Thy tail's tip is nick'd off – and though the fists
Of many a maid have given thee many a maul,
Still is that fur as soft as when the lists
In youth thou enter'dst on glass bottled wall.

John Keats

The Grasshopper and Cricket

The poetry of earth is never dead:
  When all the birds are faint with the hot sun,
  And hide in cooling trees, a voice will run
From hedge to hedge about the new-mown mead;
That is the Grasshopper's – he takes the lead
  In summer luxury – he has never done
  With his delights; for when tired out with fun
He rests at ease beneath some pleasant weed.
The poetry of earth is ceasing never:
  On a lone winter evening, when the frost
  Has wrought a silence, from the stove there shrills
The Cricket's song, in warmth increasing ever,
  And seems to one in drowsiness half lost,
    The Grasshopper's among some grassy hills.

Mary Howitt
The Spider and the Fly

"Will you walk into my parlour?" said the Spider to the Fly,
"'Tis the prettiest little parlour that ever you did spy;
The way into my parlour is up a winding stair,
And I have many curious things to show when you are there."
"Oh no, no," said the little Fly, "to ask me is in vain,
For who goes up your winding stair can ne'er come down again."

"I'm sure you must be weary, dear, with soaring up so high;
Will you rest upon my little bed?" said the Spider to the Fly.
"There are pretty curtains drawn around, the sheets are fine and thin;
And if you like to rest awhile, I'll snugly tuck you in!"
"Oh no, no," said the little Fly, "for I've often heard it said,
They never, never wake again, who sleep upon your bed!"

Said the cunning Spider to the Fly, "Dear friend, what can I do,
To prove the warm affection I've always felt for you?
I have within my pantry good store of all that's nice;
I'm sure you're very welcome – will you please to take a slice?"
"Oh no, no," said the little Fly, "kind sir, that cannot be,
I've heard what's in your pantry, and I do not wish to see."

"Sweet creature," said the Spider, "you're witty and you're wise;
How handsome are your gauzy wings, how brilliant are your eyes!
I have a little looking-glass upon my parlour shelf,
If you'll step in a moment, dear, you shall behold yourself."
"I thank you, gentle sir," she said, "for what you're pleased to say,
And bidding you good morning now, I'll call another day."

*The Spider turned him round about, and went into his
   den,
For well he knew the silly Fly would soon come back
   again;
So he wove a subtle web, in a little corner sly,
And set his table ready, to dine upon the Fly.
Then he came out to his door again, and merrily did sing:
"Come hither, hither, pretty Fly, with the pearl and
   silver wing;
Your robes are green and purple – there's a crest upon
   your head;
Your eyes are like the diamond bright, but mine are dull
   as lead."*

*Alas, alas! how very soon this silly little Fly,
Hearing his wily, flattering words, came slowly flitting
   by;
With buzzing wings she hung aloft, then near and nearer
   drew,
Thinking only of her brilliant eyes, and green and purple
   hue;*

Thinking only of her crested head – poor foolish thing! At last,
Up jumped the cunning Spider, and fiercely held her fast.
He dragged her up his winding stair, into his dismal den,
Within his little parlour – but she ne'er came out again!

Edgar Allen Poe
The Raven

Once upon a midnight dreary, while I pondered, weak and weary,
Over many a quaint and curious volume of forgotten lore –
While I nodded, nearly napping, suddenly there came a tapping,
As of some one gently rapping, rapping at my chamber door.
"'Tis some visitor," I muttered, tapping at my chamber door –
    Only this and nothing more."

Ah, distinctly I remember it was in the bleak December;
And each separate dying ember wrought its ghost upon the floor.
Eagerly I wished the morrow; – vainly I had sought to borrow
From my books surcease of sorrow – sorrow for the lost Lenore –
For the rare and radiant maiden whom the angels name Lenore –
    Nameless here for evermore.

And the silken, sad, uncertain rustling of each purple curtain
Thrilled me – filled me with fantastic terrors never felt before;
So that now, to still the beating of my heart, I stood repeating,
"'Tis some visitor entreating entrance at my chamber door; –
This it is and nothing more."

Presently my soul grew stronger; hesitating then no longer,
"Sir," said I, "or Madam, truly your forgiveness I implore;
But the fact is I was napping, and so gently you came rapping,
And so faintly you came tapping, tapping at my chamber door,
That I scarce was sure I heard you" – *here I opened wide the door; —*
Darkness there and nothing more.

Deep into that darkness peering, long I stood there wondering, fearing,
Doubting, dreaming dreams no mortal ever dared to dream before;
But the silence was unbroken, and the stillness gave no token,

*And the only word there spoken was the whispered word,
"Lenore?"*
*This I whispered, and an echo murmured back the word
"Lenore!"*
    Merely this and nothing more.

*Back into the chamber turning, all my soul within me
burning,*
Soon again I heard a tapping somewhat louder than before.
*"Surely," said I, "surely that is something at my window
lattice;*
Let me see, then, what thereat is, and this mystery explore –
Let my heart be still a moment and this mystery explore; –
    'Tis the wind and nothing more!"

*Open here I flung the shutter, when, with many a flirt and
flutter,*
In there stepped a stately Raven of the saintly days of yore;
*Not the least obeisance made he; not a minute stopped or
stayed he;*
*But, with mien of lord or lady, perched above my chamber
door –*
Perched upon a bust of Pallas just above my chamber door –
    Perched, and sat, and nothing more.

Then this ebony bird beguiling my sad fancy into smiling,
By the grave and stern decorum of the countenance it wore,
"Though thy crest be shorn and shaven, thou," I said, "art sure no craven,
Ghastly grim and ancient Raven wandering from the Nightly shore –
Tell me what thy lordly name is on the Night's Plutonian shore!"
    Quoth the Raven, "Nevermore."

Much I marvelled this ungainly fowl to hear discourse so plainly,
Though its answer little meaning – little relevancy bore;
For we cannot help agreeing that no living human being
Ever yet was blessed with seeing bird above his chamber door –
Bird or beast upon the sculptured bust above his chamber door,
    With such name as 'Nevermore.'

But the Raven, sitting lonely on the placid bust, spoke only
That one word, as if his soul in that one word he did outpour.

*Nothing farther then he uttered – not a feather then he
   fluttered –*
*Till I scarcely more than muttered, "Other friends have
   flown before –*
*On the morrow he will leave me, as my Hopes have flown
   before."*
         Then the bird said, "Nevermore."

Startled at the stillness broken by reply so aptly spoken,
*"Doubtless," said I, "what it utters is its only stock and
   store*
*Caught from some unhappy master whom unmerciful
   Disaster*
*Followed fast and followed faster till his songs one burden
   bore –*
*Till the dirges of his Hope that melancholy burden bore
         Of 'Never – nevermore.'"*

But the Raven still beguiling all my fancy into smiling,
*Straight I wheeled a cushioned seat in front of bird, and bust
   and door;*
Then, upon the velvet sinking, I betook myself to linking
Fancy unto fancy, thinking what this ominous bird of yore –

*What this grim, ungainly, ghastly, gaunt, and ominous bird
   of yore
         Meant in croaking "Nevermore."*

*This I sat engaged in guessing, but no syllable expressing
To the fowl whose fiery eyes now burned into my bosom's
   core;
This and more I sat divining, with my head at ease reclining
On the cushion's velvet lining that the lamp-light gloated
   o'er,
But whose velvet-violet lining with the lamp-light gloating
   o'er,
         She shall press, ah, nevermore!*

*Then, methought, the air grew denser, perfumed from an
   unseen censer
Swung by Seraphim whose foot-falls tinkled on the tufted
   floor.
"Wretch," I cried, "thy God hath lent thee – by these
   angels he hath sent thee
Respite – respite and nepenthe from thy memories of Lenore;
Quaff, oh, quaff this kind nepenthe and forget this lost
   Lenore!"
         Quoth the Raven, "Nevermore."*

"Prophet!" said I, "thing of evil! – prophet still, if bird or devil! –
Whether Tempter sent, or whether tempest tossed thee here ashore,
Desolate yet all undaunted, on this desert land enchanted –
On this home by Horror haunted – tell me truly, I implore –
Is there – is there balm in Gilead? – tell me – tell me, I implore!"
      Quoth the Raven, "Nevermore."

"Prophet!" said I, "thing of evil! – prophet still, if bird or devil!
By that Heaven that bends above us – by that God we both adore –
Tell this soul with sorrow laden if, within the distant Aidenn,
It shall clasp a sainted maiden whom the angels name Lenore –
Clasp a rare and radiant maiden whom the angels name Lenore."
      Quoth the Raven, "Nevermore."

"Be that word our sign of parting, bird or fiend!" I shrieked,
    upstarting –
"Get thee back into the tempest and the Night's Plutonian
    shore!
Leave no black plume as a token of that lie thy soul hath
    spoken!
Leave my loneliness unbroken! – quit the bust above my
    door!
        Quoth the Raven, "Nevermore."

And the Raven, never flitting, still is sitting, still *is* sitting
On the pallid bust of Pallas just above my chamber door;
And his eyes have all the seeming of a demon's that is
    dreaming,
And the lamp-light o'er him streaming throws his shadow on
    the floor;
And my soul from out that shadow that lies floating on the
    floor
        Shall be lifted – nevermore!

Alfred, Lord Tennyson

The Eagle

Fragment

He clasps the crag with crooked hands;
Close to the sun in lonely lands,
Ring'd with the azure world, he stands,

The wrinkled sea beneath him crawls;
He watches from his mountain walls,
And like a thunderbolt he falls.

ALFRED, LORD TENNYSON
SONG: THE OWL

When cats run home and light is come,
  And dew is cold upon the ground,
And the far-off stream is dumb,
  And the whirring sail goes round,
  And the whirring sail goes round;
    Alone and warming his five wits,
    The white owl in the belfry sits.

When merry milkmaids click the latch,
  And rarely smells the new-mown hay,
And the cock hath sung beneath the thatch
  Twice or thrice his roundelay,
  Twice or thrice his roundelay;
    Alone and warming his five wits,
    The white owl in the belfry sits.

Aunt Effie (Jane Euphemia Browne)
The Great Brown Owl

The brown owl sits in the ivy bush,
And she looketh wondrous wise,
With a horny beak beneath her cowl,
And a pair of large round eyes.

She sat all day on the selfsame spray,
From sunrise till sunset;
And the dim, grey light it was all too bright
For the owl to see in yet.

"Jenny Owlet, Jenny Owlet," said a merry little bird,
"They say you're wondrous wise;
But I don't think you see, though you're looking at me
With your large, round, shining eyes."

But night came soon, and the pale white moon
Rolled high up in the skies;
And the great brown owl flew away in her cowl,
With her large, round, shining eyes.

Edward Lear

The Duck and the Kangaroo

Said the Duck to the Kangaroo,
  "Good gracious! how you hop!
Over the fields and the water too,
  As if you never would stop!
My life is a bore in this nasty pond,
And I long to go out in the world beyond!
  I wish I could hop like you!"
  Said the Duck to the Kangaroo.

"Please give me a ride on your back!"
  Said the Duck to the Kangaroo.
"I would sit quite still, and say nothing but 'Quack',
  The whole of the long day through!
And we'd go to the Dee, and the Jelly Bo Lee,
Over the land, and over the sea;
  Please take me a ride! O do!"
  Said the Duck to the Kangaroo.

Said the Kangaroo to the Duck,
  "This requires some little reflection;
Perhaps on the whole it might bring me luck,
  And there seems but one objection,
Which is, if you'll let me speak so bold,
Your feet are unpleasantly wet and cold,
  And would probably give me the roo-
    Matiz!" said the Kangaroo.

Said the Duck, "As I sate on the rocks,
  I have thought over that completely,
And I bought four pairs of worsted socks
  Which fit my web-feet neatly.
And to keep out the cold I've bought a cloak,
And every day a cigar I'll smoke,
  All to follow my own dear true
    Love of a Kangaroo!"

Said the Kangaroo, "I'm ready!
    All in the moonlight pale;
But to balance me well, dear Duck, sit steady!
    And quite at the end of my tail!"
So away they went with a hop and a bound,
And they hopped the whole world three times round;
    And who so happy – O who,
        As the Duck and the Kangaroo?

Edward Lear
The Owl and the Pussy Cat

The Owl and the Pussy cat went to sea
  In a beautiful pea-green boat:
They took some honey, and plenty of money
  Wrapped up in a five-pound note.
The Owl looked up to the stars above,
  And sang to a small guitar,
"O lovely Pussy, O Pussy, my love,
  What a beautiful Pussy you are,
    You are,
    You are!
What a beautiful Pussy you are!"

Pussy said to the Owl, "You elegant fowl,
  How charmingly sweet you sing!
Oh! let us be married; too long we have tarried:
  But what shall we do for a ring?"
They sailed away, for a year and a day
  To the land where the bong-tree grows,
And there in a wood a Piggy-wig stood,

With a ring at the end of his nose,
   His nose,
   His nose,
With a ring at the end of his nose.

"Dear Pig, are you willing to sell for one shilling
   Your ring?" Said the Piggy, "I will."
So they took it away, and were married next day
   By the Turkey who lives on the hill.
They dinèd on mince and slices of quince,
   Which they ate with a runcible spoon,
And hand in hand, on the edge of the sand,
   They danced by the light of the moon,
     The moon,
     The moon,
   They danced by the light of the moon.

Eliza Cook

The Mouse and the Cake

A mouse found a beautiful piece of plum cake,
The richest and sweetest that mortal could make;
'Twas heavy with citron and fragrant with spice,
And covered with sugar all sparkling as ice.

"My stars!" cried the mouse, while his eye beamed with glee,
"Here's a treasure I've found: what a feast it will be;
But, hark! there's a noise, 'tis my brothers at play;
So I'll hide with the cake, lest they wander this way.

"Not a bit shall they have, for I know I can eat
Every morsel myself, and I'll have such a treat."
So off went the mouse as he held the cake fast;
While his hungry young brothers went scampering past.

He nibbled, and nibbled, and panted, but still
He kept gulping it down till he made himself ill;
Yet he swallowed it all, and 'tis easy to guess,
He was soon so unwell that he groaned with distress.

His family heard him, and as he grew worse,
They sent for the doctor, who made him rehearse
How he'd eaten the cake to the very last crumb,
Without giving his playmates and relatives some.

"Ah me!" cried the doctor, "advice is too late;
You must die before long, so prepare for your fate.
If you had but divided the cake with your brothers,
'Twould have done you no harm, and been good for the others.

"Had you shared it, the treat had been wholesome enough;
But eaten by one, *it was dangerous stuff;*
So prepare for the worst – " and the word had scarce fled,
When the doctor turned round, and the patient was dead.

Now all little people the lesson may take,
And some *large ones may learn from the mouse and the cake;*
Not to be over-selfish with what we may gain,
Or the best of our pleasures may turn into pain.

CECIL FRANCES ALEXANDER

THE FIELDMOUSE

Where the acorn tumbles down,
  Where the ash tree sheds its berry,
With your fur so soft and brown,
  With your eye so round and merry,
Scarcely moving the long grass,
Fieldmouse, I can see you pass.

Little thing, in what dark den,
  Lie you all the winter sleeping?
Till warm weather comes again,
  Then once more I see you peeping
Round about the tall tree roots,
Nibbling at their fallen fruits.

Fieldmouse, fieldmouse, do not go,
  Where the farmer stacks his treasure,
Find the nut that falls below,
  Eat the acorn at your pleasure,
But you must not steal the grain
He has stacked with so much pain.

Make your hole where mosses spring,
   Underneath the tall oak's shadow,
Pretty, quiet, harmless thing,
   Play about the sunny meadow.
Keep away from corn and house,
None will harm you, little mouse.

Emily Dickinson
A Bird Came Down the Walk

A bird came down the walk:
He did not know I saw;
He bit an angle-worm in halves
And ate the fellow, raw.

And then he drank a dew
From a convenient grass,
And then hopped sidewise to the wall
To let a beetle pass.

He glanced with rapid eyes
That hurried all abroad, –
They looked like frightened beads, I thought
He stirred his velvet head

Like one in danger; cautious,
I offered him a crumb,
And he unrolled his feathers
And rowed him softer home

Than oars divide the ocean,
Too silver for a seam,
Or butterflies, off banks of noon,
Leap, plashless, as they swim.

EMILY DICKINSON

A NARROW FELLOW IN THE GRASS

A narrow fellow in the grass
Occasionally rides;
You may have met him, – did you not?
His notice sudden is.

The grass divides as with a comb,
A spotted shaft is seen;
And then it closes at your feet
And opens further on.

He likes a boggy acre,
A floor too cool for corn.
Yet when a child, and barefoot,
I more than once, at morn,

Have passed, I thought, a whip-lash
Unbraiding in the sun, –
When, stooping to secure it,
It wrinkled, and was gone.

*Several of nature's people
I know, and they know me;
I feel for them a transport
Of cordiality;*

*But never met this fellow,
Attended or alone,
Without a tighter breathing,
And zero at the bone.*

Christina Rossetti

The Caterpillar

Brown and furry
Caterpillar in a hurry,
Take your walk
To the shady leaf, or stalk,
   Or what not,
Which may be the chosen spot.
   No toad spy you,
Hovering bird of prey pass by you;
Spin and die,
To live again as butterfly.

The Horses of the Sea

The horses of the sea
Rear a foaming crest,
But the horses of the land
Serve us best.

The horses of the land
Munch corn and clover
While the foaming sea-horses
Toss and turn over.

Lewis Carroll
How Doth the Little Crocodile

How doth the little crocodile
Improve his shining tail,
And pour the waters of the Nile
On every golden scale!

How cheerfully he seems to grin
How neatly spreads his claws,
And welcomes little fishes in,
With gently smiling jaws!

Lewis Carroll

The Walrus and the Carpenter

The sun was shining on the sea,
Shining with all his might:
He did his very best to make
The billows smooth and bright –
And this was odd, because it was
The middle of the night.

The moon was shining sulkily,
Because she thought the sun
Had got no business to be there
After the day was done –
"It's very rude of him," she said,
"To come and spoil the fun!"

The sea was wet as wet could be,
The sands were dry as dry.
You could not see a cloud, because
No cloud was in the sky:
No birds were flying overhead –
There were no birds to fly.

The Walrus and the Carpenter
Were walking close at hand:
They wept like anything to see
Such quantities of sand:
"If this were only cleared away,"
They said, "it would be grand!"

"If seven maids with seven mops
Swept it for half a year,
Do you suppose," the Walrus said,
"That they could get it clear?"
"I doubt it," said the Carpenter,
And shed a bitter tear.

"O Oysters, come and walk with us!"
The Walrus did beseech.
"A pleasant walk, a pleasant talk,
Along the briny beach:
We cannot do with more than four,
To give a hand to each."

The eldest Oyster looked at him,
But not a word he said:
The eldest Oyster winked his eye,
And shook his heavy head –
Meaning to say de did not choose
To leave the oyster-bed.

But four young Oysters hurried up,
All eager for the treat:
Their coats were brushed, their faces washed
Their shoes were clean and neat –
And this was odd, because, you know,
They hadn't any feet.

Four other Oysters followed them,
And yet another four;
And thick and fast they came at last,
And more, and more, and more –
All hopping through the frothy waves,
And scrambling to the shore.

The Walrus and the Carpenter
Walked on a mile or so,
And then they rested on a rock
Conveniently low:
And all the little Oysters stood
And waited in a row.

"The time has come," the Walrus said,
"To talk of many things:
Of shoes – and ships – and sealing wax –
Of cabbages – and kings –
And why the sea is boiling hot –
And whether pigs have wings."

"But wait a bit," the Oysters cried,
"Before we have our chat;
For some of us are out of breath,
And all of us are fat!"
"No hurry!" said the Carpenter.
They thanked him much for that.

"A loaf of bread," the Walrus said,
"Is what we chiefly need:
Pepper and vinegar besides
Are very good indeed –
Now, if you're ready, Oysters dear,
We can begin to feed."

"But not on us!" the Oysters cried,
Turning a little blue.
"After such kindness that would be
A dismal thing to do!"
"The night is fine," the Walrus said,
"Do you admire the view?

"It was so kind of you to come,
And you are very nice!"
The Carpenter said nothing but
"Cut us another slice.
I wish you were not quite so deaf –
I've had to ask you twice!"

"It seems a shame," the Walrus said,
"To play them such a trick.
After we've brought them out so far,
And made them trot so quick!"
The Carpenter said nothing but
"The butter's spread too thick!"

"I weep for you," the Walrus said:
"I deeply sympathise."
With sobs and tears he sorted out
Those of the largest size,
Holding his pocket-handkerchief
Before his streaming eyes.

"O Oysters," said the Carpenter,
"You've had a pleasant run!
Shall we be trotting home again?"
But answer came there none –
And this was scarcely odd, because
They'd eaten every one.

RICHARD GARNETT

MARIGOLD

She moved through the garden in glory because
She had very long claws at the end of her paws.
Her back was arched, her tail was high,
A green fire glared in her vivid eye;
And all the Toms, though never so bold,
Quailed at the martial Marigold.

Thomas Hardy

The Oxen

Christmas Eve, and twelve of the clock.
"Now they are all on their knees,"
An elder said as we sat in a flock
By the embers in hearthside ease.

We pictured the meek mild creatures where
They dwelt in their strawy pen,
Nor did it occur to one of us there
To doubt they were kneeling then.

So fair a fancy few would weave
In these years! Yet, I feel,
If someone said on Christmas Eve,
"Come; see the oxen kneel

"In the lonely barton by yonder coomb
Our childhood used to know,"
I should go with him in the gloom,
Hoping it might be so.

CHARLES E. CARRYL
THE CAMEL'S COMPLAINT

Canary-birds feed on sugar and seed,
   Parrots have crackers to crunch;
And as for the poodles, they tell me the noodles
   Have chicken and cream for their lunch.
      But there's never a question
      About my digestion –
         Anything *does* for me.

Cats, you're aware, can repose in a chair,
   Chickens can roost upon rails;
Puppies are able to sleep in a stable,
   And oysters can slumber in pails.
      But no one supposes
      A poor Camel dozes –
         Any place *does* for me.

Lambs are enclosed where it's never exposed,
   Coops are constructed for hens;
Kittens are treated to houses well heated,
   And pigs are protected by pens.

*But a camel comes handy
Wherever it's sandy –
　Anywhere does for me.*

People would laugh if you rode a giraffe,
　Or mounted the back of an ox;
It's nobody's habit to ride on a rabbit,
　Or try to bestraddle a fox.
　　But as for a camel, he's
　　Ridden by families –
　　　Any load *does for me.*

A snake is as round as a hole in the ground,
　And weasels are wavy and sleek;
And no alligator could ever be straighter
　Than lizards that live in a creek.
　　But a camel's all lumpy
　　And bumpy and humpy –
　　　Any shape *does for me.*

A.E. Housman

The Elephant, or The Force of Habit

A tail behind, a trunk in front,
Complete the usual elephant.
The tail in front, the trunk behind
Is what you very seldom find.

If you for specimens should hunt
With trunks behind and tails in front,
That hunt would occupy you long;
The force of habit is so strong.

Kenneth Grahame
Ducks' Ditty

All along the backwater,
Through the rushes tall,
Ducks are a-dabbling,
Up tails all!

Ducks' tails, drakes' tails,
Yellow feet a-quiver,
Yellow bills all out of sight
Busy in the river!

Slushy green undergrowth
Where the roach swim –
Here we keep our larder,
Cool and full and dim!

Every one for what he likes!
We like to be
Heads down, tails up,
Dabbling free!

*High in the blue above
Swifts whirl and call –
We are down a-dabbling
Up tails all!*

JOHN DAVIDSON

A RUNNABLE STAG

When the pods went pop on the broom, green broom,
  And apples began to be golden-skinned,
We harboured a stag in the Priory coomb,
  And we feathered his trail up-wind, up-wind,
  We feathered his trail up-wind –
    A stag of warrant, a stag, a stag,
    A runnable stag, a kingly crop,
    Brow, bay and tray and three on top,
    A stag, a runnable stag.

Then the huntsman's horn rang yap, yap, yap,
  And 'Forwards' we heard the harbourer shout;
But 'twas only a brocket that broke a gap
  In the beechen underwood, driven out,
  From the underwood antlered out
    By warrant and might of the stag, the stag,
    The runnable stag, whose lordly mind
    Was bent on sleep, though beamed and tined
    He stood, a runnable stag.

So we tufted the covert till afternoon
   With Tinkerman's Pup and Bell-of-the-North;
And hunters were sulky and hounds out of tune
   Before we tufted the right stag forth,
   Before we tufted him forth,
     The stag of warrant, the wily stag,
     The runnable stag with his kingly crop,
     Brow, bay and tray and three on top,
     The royal and runnable stag.

It was Bell-of-the-North and Tinkerman's Pup
   That stuck to the scent till the copse was drawn.
'Tally ho! tally ho!' and the hunt was up,
   The tufters whipped and the pack laid on,
   The resolute pack laid on,
     And the stag of warrant away at last,
     The runnable stag, the same, the same,
     His hoofs on fire, his horns like flame,
     A stag, a runnable stag.

"Let your gelding be: if you check or chide
    He stumbles at once and you're out of the hunt;
For three hundred gentlemen, able to ride,
    On hunters accustomed to bear the brunt,
    Accustomed to bear the brunt,
        Are after the runnable stag, the stag,
        The runnable stag with his kingly crop,
        Brow, bay and tray and three on top,
        The right, the runnable stag."

By perilous paths in coomb and dell,
    The heather, the rocks, and the river-bed,
The pace grew hot, for the scent lay well,
    And a runnable stag goes right ahead,
    The quarry went right ahead –
        Ahead, ahead, and fast and far;
        His antlered crest, his cloven hoof,
        Brow, bay and tray and three aloof,
        The stag, the runnable stag.

For a matter of twenty miles and more,
   By the densest hedge and the highest wall,
Through herds of bullocks he baffled the lore
   Of harbourer, huntsman, hounds and all,
   Of harbourer hounds and all –
      The stag of warrant, the wily stag,
      For twenty miles, and five and five,
      He ran, and he never was caught alive,
      This stag, this runnable stag.

When he turned at bay in the leafy gloom,
   In the emerald gloom where the brook ran deep,
He heard in the distance the rollers boom,
   And he saw in a vision of peaceful sleep,
   In a wonderful vision of sleep,
      A stag of warrant, a stag, a stag,
      A runnable stag in a jewelled bed,
      Under the sheltering ocean dead,
      A stag, a runnable stag.

So a fateful hope lit up his eye,
  And he opened his nostrils wide again,
And he tossed his branching antlers high
  As he headed the hunt down the Charlock glen,
  As he raced down the echoing glen
    For five miles more, the glen, the stag,
    For twenty miles, and five and five,
    Not to be caught now, dead or alive,
    The stag, the runnable stag.

Three hundred gentlemen, able to ride,
  Three hundred horses as gallant and free,
Beheld him escape on the evening tide,
  Far out till he sank in the Severn Sea,
  Till he sank in the depths of the sea –
    The stag, the buoyant stag, the stag
    That slept at last in a jewelled bed
    Under the sheltering ocean spread,
    The stag, the runnable stag.

Rudyard Kipling

The Law of the Jungle

Now this is the Law of the Jungle – as old and as true as the sky;
And the Wolf that shall keep it may prosper, but the Wolf that shall break it must die.

As the creeper that girdles the tree-trunk the Law runneth forward and back –
For the strength of the Pack is the Wolf, and the strength of the Wolf is the Pack.

Wash daily from nose-tip to tail-tip; drink deeply, but never too deep;
And remember the night is for hunting, and forget not the day is for sleep.

The Jackal may follow the Tiger, but, Cub, when thy whiskers are grown,
Remember the Wolf is a hunter – go forth and get food of thine own.

*Keep peace with the Lords of the Jungle – the Tiger, the
    Panther, the Bear;
And trouble not Hathi the Silent, and mock not the Boar in
    his lair.*

*When Pack meets with Pack in the Jungle, and neither will
    go from the trail,
Lie down till the leaders have spoken – it may be fair words
    shall prevail.*

*When ye fight with a Wolf of the Pack, ye must fight him
    alone and afar,
Lest others take part in the quarrel, and the Pack be
    diminished by war.*

*The Lair of the Wolf is his refuge, and where he has made
    him his home,
Not even the Head Wolf may enter, not even the Council
    may come.*

*The Lair of the Wolf is his refuge, but where he has digged
    it too plain,
The Council shall send him a message, and so he shall
    change it again.*

If ye kill before midnight, be silent, and wake not the woods with your bay,
Lest ye frighten the deer from the crops, and the brothers go empty away.

Ye may kill for yourselves, and your mates, and your cubs as they need, and ye can;
But kill not for pleasure of killing, and seven times never kill Man!

If ye plunder his Kill from a weaker, devour not all in thy pride;
Pack-Right is the right of the meanest; so leave him the head and the hide.

The Kill of the Pack is the meat of the Pack. Ye must eat where it lies;
And no one may carry away of that meat to his lair, or he dies.

The Kill of the Wolf is the meat of the Wolf. He may do what he will,
But, till he has given permission, the Pack may not eat of that Kill.

Cub-Right is the right of the Yearling. From all of his Pack he may claim
Full-gorge when the killer has eaten; and none may refuse him the same.

Lair-Right is the right of the Mother. From all of her year she may claim
One haunch of each kill for her litter; and none may deny her the same.

Cave-Right is the right of the Father – to hunt by himself for his own:
He is freed of all calls to the Pack; he is judged by the Council alone.

Because of his age and his cunning, because of his gripe and his paw,
In all that the Law leaveth open, the word of the Head Wolf is Law.

Now these are the Laws of the Jungle, and many and mighty are they;
But the head and the hoof of the Law and the haunch and the hump is – Obey!

Rudyard Kipling
How the Camel Got His Hump

The Camel's hump is any ugly lump
  Which well you may see at the Zoo;
But uglier yet is the hump we get
  From having too little to do.

Kiddies and grown-ups too-oo-oo,
If we haven't enough to do-oo-oo,
    We get the hump –
    Cameelious hump –
The hump that is black and blue!

We climb out of bed with a frouzly head,
  And a snarly-yarly voice.
We shiver and scowl and we grunt and we growl
  At our bath and our boots and our toys;

And there ought to be a corner for me
(And I know there is one for you)
    When we get the hump –
    Cameelious hump –
The hump that is black and blue!

The cure for this ill is not to sit still,
  Or frowst with a book by the fire;
But to take a large hoe and a shovel also,
  And dig till you gently perspire;

And then you will find that the sun and the wind,
And the Djinn of the Garden too,
    Have lifted the hump –
    The horrible hump –
The hump that is black and blue!

I get it as well as you-oo-oo –
If I haven't enough to do-oo-oo!
    We all get hump –
    Cameelious hump –
Kiddies and grown-ups too!

Rudyard Kipling

From: The Cat That Walked by Himself

Pussy can sit by the fire and sing,
Pussy can climb a tree,
Or play with a silly old cork and string
To 'muse herself, not me.
But I like Binkie my dog, because
He knows how to behave;
So, Binkie's the same as the First Friend was,
And I am the Man in the Cave!

Pussy will play man-Friday till
It's time to wet her paw
And make her walk on the window-sill
(For the footprint Crusoe saw);
Then she fluffles her tail and mews,
And scratches and won't attend.
But Binkie will play whatever I choose,
And he is my true First Friend!

*Pussy will rub my knees with her head
Pretending she loves me hard;
But the very minute I go to my bed
Pussy runs out in the yard,
And there she stays till the morning-light;
So I know it is only pretend;
But* Binkie, *he snores at my feet all night,
And he is my Firstest Friend!*

W.B. Yeats

The Cat and the Moon

The cat went here and there
And the moon spun round like a top,
And the nearest kin of the moon,
The creeping cat, looked up.
Black Minnaloushe stared at the moon,
For, wander and wail as he would,
The pure cold light in the sky
Troubled his animal blood.
Minnaloushe runs in the grass
Lifting his delicate feet.
Do you dance, Minnaloushe, do you dance?
When two close kindred meet,
What better than call a dance?
Maybe the moon may learn,
Tired of that courtly fashion,
A new dance turn.
Minnaloushe creeps through the grass
From moonlit place to place,
The sacred moon overhead
Has taken a new phase.
Does Minnaloushe know that his pupils

Will pass from change to change,
And that from round to crescent,
From crescent to round they range?
Minnaloushe creeps through the grass
Alone, important and wise,
And lifts to the changing moon
His changing eyes.

W.B. Yeats

The Wild Swans at Coole

The trees are in their autumn beauty,
The woodland paths are dry,
Under the October twilight the water
Mirrors a still sky;
Upon the brimming water among the stones
Are nine and fifty swans.

The nineteenth Autumn has come upon me
Since I first made my count;
I saw, before I had well finished,
All suddenly mount
And scatter, wheeling, in great broken rings
Upon their clamorous wings.

I have looked upon those brilliant creatures,
And now my heart is sore.
All's changed since I, hearing at twilight,
The first time on this shore,
The bell-beat of their wings above my head,
Trod with a lighter tread.

Unwearied still, lover by lover,
They paddle in the cold,
Companionable streams or climb the air;
Their hearts have not grown old;
Passion or conquest, wander where they will,
Attend upon them still.

But now they drift on the still water
Mysterious, beautiful;
Among what rushes will they build,
By what lake's edge or pool
Delight men's eyes, when I awake some day
To find they have flown away?

G.K. Chesterton

The Donkey

When fishes flew and forests walked,
And figs grew upon thorn,
Some moments when the moon was blood,
Then surely I was born;

With monstrous head and sickening cry
And ears like errant wings,
The devil's walking parody
On all four-footed things.

The tattered outlaw of the earth,
Of ancient crooked will;
Starve, scourge, deride me; I am dumb,
I keep my secret still.

Fools! For I also had my hour;
One far fierce hour and sweet;
There was a shout about my ears,
And palms before my feet.

G.K. Chesterton
Triolet

I wish I were a jelly fish
That cannot fall downstairs:
Of all the things I wish to wish
I wish I were a jelly fish
That hasn't any cares,
And doesn't even have to wish
"I wish I were a jelly fish
That cannot fall downstairs."

Vachel Lindsay

The Flower-fed Buffaloes

The flower-fed buffaloes of the spring
In the days of long ago,
Ranged where the locomotives sing
And the prairie flowers lie low: –
The tossing, blooming, perfumed grass
Is swept away by the wheat,
Wheels and wheels and wheels spin by
In the spring that still is sweet.
But the flower-fed buffaloes of the spring
Left us, long ago.
They gore no more, they bellow no more,
They trundle around the hills no more: –
With the Blackfeet, lying low,
With the Pawnees, lying low,
Lying low.

JOHN DRINKWATER
SNAIL

Snail upon the wall,
Have you got at all
Anything to tell
About your shell?

Only this, my child –
When the wind is wild,
Or when the sun is hot,
It's all I've got.

D.H. Lawrence

Humming-bird

I can imagine, in some otherworld
Primeval – dumb, far back
In that most awful stillness that only gasped and hummed,
Humming-birds raced down the avenues.

Before anything had a soul,
While life was a heave of Matter, half inanimate,
This little bit chipped off in brilliance
And went whizzing through the slow, vast, succulent stems.

I believe there were no flowers then,
In the world where the humming-bird flashed ahead of creation,
I believe he pierced the slow vegetable veins with his long beak.
Probably he was big
As mosses and little lizards, they say, were once big.
Probably he was a jabbing, terrifying monster.

We look at him through the wrong end of the long telescope of Time,
Luckily for us.

D.H. Lawrence

Snake

A snake came to my water-trough
On a hot, hot day, and I in pyjamas for the heat,
To drink there.

In the deep, strange-scented shade of the great dark carob-tree
I came down the steps with my pitcher
And must wait, must stand and wait, for there he was at the trough before me.

He reached down from a fissure in the earth-wall in the gloom
And trailed his yellow-brown slackness soft-bellied down, over the edge of the stone trough
And rested his throat upon the stone bottom,
And where the water had dripped from the tap, in a small clearness,
He sipped with his straight mouth,
Softly drank through his straight gums, into his slack long body,
Silently.

Someone was before me at my water-trough,
And I, like a second comer, waiting.
He lifted his head from his drinking, as cattle do,
And looked at me vaguely, as drinking cattle do,
And flickered his two-forked tongue from his lips, and mused a moment,
And stooped and drank a little more,
Being earth-brown, earth-golden from the burning bowels of the earth
On the day of Sicilian July, with Etna smoking.

The voice of my education said to me
He must be killed,
For in Sicily the black, black snakes are innocent, the gold are venomous.

And voices in me said, If you were a man
You would take a stick and break him now, and finish him off.

But must I confess how I liked him,
How glad I was he had come like a guest in quiet, to drink at my water-trough
And depart peaceful, pacified, and thankless,

Into the burning bowels of this earth?

Was it cowardice, that I dared not kill him?
Was it perversity, that I longed to talk to him?
Was it humility, to feel so honoured?
I felt so honoured.
And yet those voices:
If you were not afraid, you would kill him!

And truly I was afraid, I was most afraid,
But even so, honoured still more
That he should seek my hospitality
From out the dark door of the secret earth.

He drank enough
And lifted his head, dreamily, as one who has drunken,
And flickered his tongue like a forked night on the air so black,
Seeming to lick his lips,
And looked around like a god, unseeing, into the air,
And slowly turned his head,
And slowly, very slowly, as if thrice adream,
Proceeded to draw his slow length curving round
And climb again the broken bank of my wall-face.

And as he put his head into that dreadful hole,
*And as he slowly drew up, snake-easing his shoulders, and
    entered farther,*
*A sort of horror, a sort of protest against his withdrawing
    into that horrid black hole,*
*Deliberately going into the blackness, and slowly drawing
    himself after,*
Overcame me now his back was turned.
I looked round, I put down my pitcher,
I picked up a clumsy log
And threw it at the water-trough with a clatter.

I think it did not hit him,
*But suddenly that part of him that was left behind convulsed
    in undignified haste,*
Writhed like lightning, and was gone
Into the black hole, the earth-lipped fissure in the wall-front,
At which, in the intense still noon, I stared with fascination.

And immediately I regretted it.
I thought how paltry, how vulgar, what a mean act!
I despised myself and the voices of my accursed human
  education.
And I thought of the albatross,
And I wished he would come back, my snake.

For he seemed to me again like a king,
Like a king in exile, uncrowned in the underworld,
Now due to be crowned again.

And so, I missed my chance with one of the lords
Of Life.
And I have something to expiate;
A pettiness.

Humbert Wolfe
The Blackbird

*In the far corner
close by the swings,
every morning
a blackbird sings.*

*His bill's so yellow,
His coat's so black,
that he makes a fellow
whistle back.*

*Ann, my daughter,
thinks that he
sings for us two
especially.*

Humbert Wolfe
The Grey Squirrel

Like a small grey
coffee-pot
sits the squirrel.
He is not
all he should be,
kills by dozens
trees, and eats
his red-brown cousins.

The keeper, on the
other hand,
who shot him, is
a Christian, and

loves his enemies,
which shows
the squirrel was not
one of those.

Elizabeth Madox Roberts
The Hens

The night was coming very fast;
It reached the gate as I ran past.

The pigeons had gone to the tower of the church
And all the hens were on their perch,

Up in the barn, and I thought I heard
A piece of a little purring word.

I stopped inside, waiting and staying,
To try to hear what the hens were saying.

They were asking something, that was plain,
Asking it over and over again.

One of them moved and turned around,
Her feathers made a ruffled sound,

A ruffled sound, like a bushful of birds,
And she said her little asking words.

She pushed her head close into her wing,
But nothing answered anything.

Julian Grenfell
To a Black Greyhound

Shining black in the shining light,
  Inky black in the golden sun,
Graceful as the swallow's flight,
  Light as swallow, wingèd one,
Swift as driven hurricane –
  Double-sinewed stretch and spring,
Muffled thud of flying feet,
  See the black dog galloping,
  Hear his wild foot-beat.

See him lie when the day is dead,
  Black curves curled on the boarded floor.
Sleepy eyes, my sleepy-head –
  Eyes that were aflame before.
Gentle now, they burn no more;
  Gentle now and softly warm,
With the fire that made them bright
  Hidden – as when after storm
  Softly falls the night.

God of speed, who makes the fire –
   God of Peace, who lulls the same –
God who gives the fierce desire,
   Lust for blood as fierce as flame –
God who stands in Pity's name –
   Many may ye be or less,
Ye who rule the earth and sun:
   Gods of strength and gentleness,
   Ye are ever one.